DOGMA

A Dog's Guide to Life

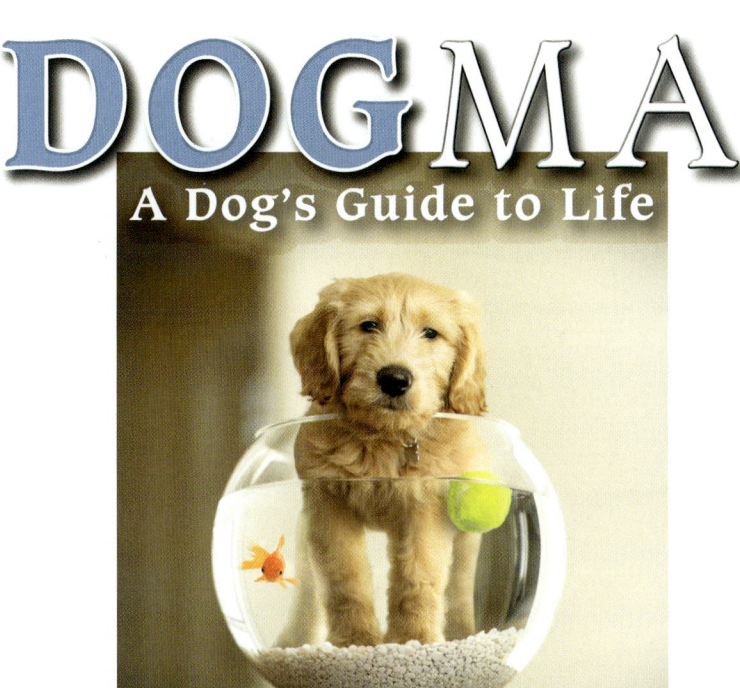

16-MONTH WEEKLY PLANNER
September 2020 – December 2021

If Lost Please Return To:

S0-FBC-888

☎ _____

✉ _____

⌂ _____

_____

_____

Published by Sellers Publishing, Inc.
For more information regarding this and other products:
WWW.MAKEFUN.COM I RSP@RSVP.COM
Canadian Stores Contact: Andrew Shapiro
(800) 625-3386 I ASHAPIRO@RSVP.COM

Astronomical information is in Eastern Time and Daylight Saving Time.
Key to abbreviations: United States (US), Canada (CAN), United Kingdom (UK), Australia (AUS), South Australia (SA), Western Australia (W. Australia), New South Wales (NSW), Australian Capital Territory (ACT), New Zealand (NZ).

If you've got a song to sing
— sing it!

2020

JANUARY
S	M	T	W	T	F	S
			1	2	3	4
5	6	7	8	9	10	11
12	13	14	15	16	17	18
19	20	21	22	23	24	25
26	27	28	29	30	31	

FEBRUARY
S	M	T	W	T	F	S
						1
2	3	4	5	6	7	8
9	10	11	12	13	14	15
16	17	18	19	20	21	22
23	24	25	26	27	28	29

MARCH
S	M	T	W	T	F	S
1	2	3	4	5	6	7
8	9	10	11	12	13	14
15	16	17	18	19	20	21
22	23	24	25	26	27	28
29	30	31				

APRIL
S	M	T	W	T	F	S
			1	2	3	4
5	6	7	8	9	10	11
12	13	14	15	16	17	18
19	20	21	22	23	24	25
26	27	28	29	30		

MAY
S	M	T	W	T	F	S
					1	2
3	4	5	6	7	8	9
10	11	12	13	14	15	16
17	18	19	20	21	22	23
24	25	26	27	28	29	30
31						

JUNE
S	M	T	W	T	F	S
	1	2	3	4	5	6
7	8	9	10	11	12	13
14	15	16	17	18	19	20
21	22	23	24	25	26	27
28	29	30				

JULY
S	M	T	W	T	F	S
			1	2	3	4
5	6	7	8	9	10	11
12	13	14	15	16	17	18
19	20	21	22	23	24	25
26	27	28	29	30	31	

AUGUST
S	M	T	W	T	F	S
						1
2	3	4	5	6	7	8
9	10	11	12	13	14	15
16	17	18	19	20	21	22
23	24	25	26	27	28	29
30	31					

SEPTEMBER
S	M	T	W	T	F	S
		1	2	3	4	5
6	7	8	9	10	11	12
13	14	15	16	17	18	19
20	21	22	23	24	25	26
27	28	29	30			

OCTOBER
S	M	T	W	T	F	S
				1	2	3
4	5	6	7	8	9	10
11	12	13	14	15	16	17
18	19	20	21	22	23	24
25	26	27	28	29	30	31

NOVEMBER
S	M	T	W	T	F	S
1	2	3	4	5	6	7
8	9	10	11	12	13	14
15	16	17	18	19	20	21
22	23	24	25	26	27	28
29	30					

DECEMBER
S	M	T	W	T	F	S
		1	2	3	4	5
6	7	8	9	10	11	12
13	14	15	16	17	18	19
20	21	22	23	24	25	26
27	28	29	30	31		

September
2020

AUGUST
S M T W T F S
1
2 3 4 5 6 7 8
9 10 11 12 13 14 15
16 17 18 19 20 21 22
23 24 25 26 27 28 29
30 31

OCTOBER
S M T W T F S
1 2 3
4 5 6 7 8 9 10
11 12 13 14 15 16 17
18 19 20 21 22 23 24
25 26 27 28 29 30 31

Sunday	Monday	Tuesday	Wednesday	Thursday	Friday	Saturday
30	31	1	2 ○ FULL MOON	3	4	5
6 Father's Day (Australia, NZ)	7 Labor Day (US, Canada)	8	9	10	11	12
13	14	15	16	17 ● NEW MOON	18 Rosh Hashanah begins at sundown	19
20	21 UN International Day of Peace	22 Autumnal Equinox	23	24	25	26
27 Yom Kippur begins at sundown	28 Queen's Birthday (W. Australia)	29	30	1	2	3

Don't be afraid to make a splash.

_____
_____
_____
_____
_____
_____
_____
_____
_____
_____
_____

| 31 | Monday | Bank Holiday (UK) |

| 1 | Tuesday | |

| 2 | Wednesday | ○ FULL MOON |

| 3 | Thursday | |

| 4 | Friday | |

| 5 | Saturday | |

| 6 | Sunday | Father's Day (Australia, NZ) |

2020

When inspiration calls, listen carefully.

September

7	Monday	Labor Day (US, Canada)
8	Tuesday	
9	Wednesday	
10	Thursday	
11	Friday	
12	Saturday	
13	Sunday	

2020

Be prepared to bring home the bacon.

September

14	Monday

15	Tuesday

16	Wednesday

17	Thursday	● NEW MOON

18	Friday	Rosh Hashanah begins at sundown

19	Saturday

20	Sunday

2020

Be happy with who you are.

September

21	Monday	UN International Day of Peace
22	Tuesday	Autumnal Equinox
23	Wednesday	
24	Thursday	
25	Friday	
26	Saturday	
27	Sunday	Yom Kippur begins at sundown

2020

October
2020

SEPTEMBER
S M T W T F S
1 2 3 4 5
6 7 8 9 10 11 12
13 14 15 16 17 18 19
20 21 22 23 24 25 26
27 28 29 30

NOVEMBER
S M T W T F S
1 2 3 4 5 6 7
8 9 10 11 12 13 14
15 16 17 18 19 20 21
22 23 24 25 26 27 28
29 30

Sunday	Monday	Tuesday	Wednesday	Thursday	Friday	Saturday
27	28	29	30	1 ○ FULL MOON	2	3
4	5 Labour Day (ACT, NSW, SA) Queen's Birthday (Queensland)	6	7	8	9	10
11	12 Columbus Day (observed) Thanksgiving (Canada) Indigenous Peoples' Day (observed)	13	14	15	16 ● NEW MOON	17
18	19	20	21	22	23	24
25	26 Labour Day (New Zealand)	27	28	29	30	31 Halloween ○ FULL MOON

NOTES

*Life is unpredictable —
eat dessert first.*

_____

_____

_____

_____

_____

_____

_____

_____

_____

_____

September /
October

| 28 | Monday | Queen's Birthday (W. Australia) |

| 29 | Tuesday | |

| 30 | Wednesday | |

| 1 | Thursday | ○ FULL MOON |

| 2 | Friday | |

| 3 | Saturday | |

| 4 | Sunday | |

2020

Don't let anyone burst your bubble.

October

5	Monday	Labour Day (ACT, NSW, SA) Queen's Birthday (Queensland)
6	Tuesday	
7	Wednesday	
8	Thursday	
9	Friday	
10	Saturday	
11	Sunday	

2020

Your heart knows the way —
follow it.

October

12	Monday	Columbus Day (observed)
		Thanksgiving (Canada)
		Indigenous Peoples' Day (observed)

13 | Tuesday

14 | Wednesday

15 | Thursday

16 | Friday ⚫ NEW MOON

17 | Saturday

18 | Sunday

2020

Be careful, but don't be ridiculous.

October

19	Monday
20	Tuesday
21	Wednesday
22	Thursday
23	Friday
24	Saturday
25	Sunday

2020

November
2020

OCTOBER
S M T W T F S
1 2 3
4 5 6 7 8 9 10
11 12 13 14 15 16 17
18 19 20 21 22 23 24
25 26 27 28 29 30 31

DECEMBER
S M T W T F S
1 2 3 4 5
6 7 8 9 10 11 12
13 14 15 16 17 18 19
20 21 22 23 24 25 26
27 28 29 30 31

Sunday	Monday	Tuesday	Wednesday	Thursday	Friday	Saturday
1 All Saints' Day Daylight Saving ends	2	3 Election Day	4	5	6	7
8 Remembrance Sunday (UK)	9	10	11 Veterans Day Remembrance Day (CAN, AUS, NZ)	12	13	14
15 ● NEW MOON	16	17	18	19	20	21
22	23	24	25	26 Thanksgiving	27	28
29	30 ○ FULL MOON	1	2	3	4	5

Knee-high or up to your neck —
it all depends on your perspective.

| 26 | Monday | Labour Day (New Zealand) |

| 27 | Tuesday | |

| 28 | Wednesday | |

| 29 | Thursday | |

| 30 | Friday | |

| 31 | Saturday | Halloween
 ○ FULL MOON |

| 1 | Sunday | All Saints' Day
 Daylight Saving ends |

*An honest day's work makes
for a good night's sleep.*

_____

_____

_____

_____

_____

_____

_____

_____

_____

_____

November

2	Monday	

3	Tuesday	Election Day

4	Wednesday	

5	Thursday	

6	Friday	

7	Saturday	

8	Sunday	Remembrance Sunday (UK)

2020

Life is a journey — good friends make the
ride more fun.

November

9	Monday

10	Tuesday

11	Wednesday	Veterans Day
		Remembrance Day (CAN, AUS, NZ)

12	Thursday

13	Friday

14	Saturday

15	Sunday	● NEW MOON

2020

Seize the moments that make life sweet.

November

16	Monday
17	Tuesday
18	Wednesday
19	Thursday
20	Friday
21	Saturday
22	Sunday

2020

Know your competition.

November

23	Monday	
24	Tuesday	
25	Wednesday	
26	Thursday	Thanksgiving
27	Friday	
28	Saturday	
29	Sunday	

2020

December
2020

NOVEMBER
S M T W T F S
1 2 3 4 5 6 7
8 9 10 11 12 13 14
15 16 17 18 19 20 21
22 23 24 25 26 27 28
29 30

JANUARY 2021
S M T W T F S
1 2
3 4 5 6 7 8 9
10 11 12 13 14 15 16
17 18 19 20 21 22 23
24 25 26 27 28 29 30
31

Sunday	Monday	Tuesday	Wednesday	Thursday	Friday	Saturday
29	30	1	2	3	4	5
6	7 Pearl Harbor Remembrance Day	8	9	10 Hanukkah begins at sundown	11	12
13	14 ● NEW MOON	15	16	17	18	19
20	21 Winter Solstice	22	23	24	25 Christmas	26 Boxing Day (CAN, UK, AUS, NZ) Kwanzaa begins
27	28 Boxing Day (observed) (CAN, UK, AUS, NZ)	29 ○ FULL MOON	30	31	1	2

NOTES

Good things are worth waiting for.

| 30 | Monday | ○ FULL MOON |

| 1 | Tuesday |

| 2 | Wednesday |

| 3 | Thursday |

| 4 | Friday |

| 5 | Saturday |

| 6 | Sunday |

Some are born beautiful.
The rest of us have to work at it.

December

7	Monday	
8	Tuesday	
9	Wednesday	
10	Thursday	Hanukkah begins at sundown
11	Friday	
12	Saturday	
13	Sunday	

2020

Learn to cover your tracks.

December

| 14 | Monday | ● NEW MOON |

| 15 | Tuesday |

| 16 | Wednesday |

| 17 | Thursday |

| 18 | Friday |

| 19 | Saturday |

| 20 | Sunday |

2020

Start your own traditions.

December

21	Monday	<div align="right">Winter Solstice</div>
22	Tuesday	
23	Wednesday	
24	Thursday	
25	Friday	<div align="right">Christmas</div>
26	Saturday	<div align="right">Kwanzaa begins Boxing Day (CAN, UK, AUS, NZ)</div>
27	Sunday	

2020

January
2021

Sunday	Monday	Tuesday	Wednesday	Thursday	Friday	Saturday
27	28	29	30	31	1 New Year's Day	2
3	4	5	6	7	8	9
10	11	12	13 ● NEW MOON	14	15 Martin Luther King Jr.'s Birthday	16
17	18 Martin Luther King Jr.'s Birthday (observed)	19	20	21	22	23
24/31	25	26 Australia Day	27	28 ○ FULL MOON	29	30

2021

JANUARY

S	M	T	W	T	F	S
					1	2
3	4	5	6	7	8	9
10	11	12	13	14	15	16
17	18	19	20	21	22	23
24	25	26	27	28	29	30
31						

FEBRUARY

S	M	T	W	T	F	S
	1	2	3	4	5	6
7	8	9	10	11	12	13
14	15	16	17	18	19	20
21	22	23	24	25	26	27
28						

MARCH

S	M	T	W	T	F	S
	1	2	3	4	5	6
7	8	9	10	11	12	13
14	15	16	17	18	19	20
21	22	23	24	25	26	27
28	29	30	31			

APRIL

S	M	T	W	T	F	S
				1	2	3
4	5	6	7	8	9	10
11	12	13	14	15	16	17
18	19	20	21	22	23	24
25	26	27	28	29	30	

MAY

S	M	T	W	T	F	S
						1
2	3	4	5	6	7	8
9	10	11	12	13	14	15
16	17	18	19	20	21	22
23	24	25	26	27	28	29
30	31					

JUNE

S	M	T	W	T	F	S
		1	2	3	4	5
6	7	8	9	10	11	12
13	14	15	16	17	18	19
20	21	22	23	24	25	26
27	28	29	30			

JULY

S	M	T	W	T	F	S
				1	2	3
4	5	6	7	8	9	10
11	12	13	14	15	16	17
18	19	20	21	22	23	24
25	26	27	28	29	30	31

AUGUST

S	M	T	W	T	F	S
1	2	3	4	5	6	7
8	9	10	11	12	13	14
15	16	17	18	19	20	21
22	23	24	25	26	27	28
29	30	31				

SEPTEMBER

S	M	T	W	T	F	S
			1	2	3	4
5	6	7	8	9	10	11
12	13	14	15	16	17	18
19	20	21	22	23	24	25
26	27	28	29	30		

OCTOBER

S	M	T	W	T	F	S
					1	2
3	4	5	6	7	8	9
10	11	12	13	14	15	16
17	18	19	20	21	22	23
24	25	26	27	28	29	30
31						

NOVEMBER

S	M	T	W	T	F	S
	1	2	3	4	5	6
7	8	9	10	11	12	13
14	15	16	17	18	19	20
21	22	23	24	25	26	27
28	29	30				

DECEMBER

S	M	T	W	T	F	S
			1	2	3	4
5	6	7	8	9	10	11
12	13	14	15	16	17	18
19	20	21	22	23	24	25
26	27	28	29	30	31	

Be prepared for any situation.

| 28 | Monday | Boxing Day (observed)
(CAN, UK, AUS, NZ) |

| 29 | Tuesday | ○ FULL MOON |

| 30 | Wednesday | |

| 31 | Thursday | |

| 1 | Friday | New Year's Day |

| 2 | Saturday | |

| 3 | Sunday | |

Enjoy all the sweetness life has to offer.

January

4	Monday

5	Tuesday

6	Wednesday

7	Thursday

8	Friday

9	Saturday

10	Sunday

2021

Don't be afraid to blaze new trails.

January

11	Monday

12	Tuesday

13	Wednesday	● NEW MOON

14	Thursday

15	Friday	Martin Luther King Jr.'s Birthday

16	Saturday

17	Sunday

2021

Dream big and stay on your toes.

January

18	Monday	<div align="right">Martin Luther King Jr.'s Birthday (observed)</div>
19	Tuesday	
20	Wednesday	
21	Thursday	
22	Friday	
23	Saturday	
24	Sunday	

2021

Enthusiasm will help you lick any task.

_____

_____

_____

_____

_____

_____

_____

_____

_____

_____

_____

January

25	Monday	
26	Tuesday	Australia Day
27	Wednesday	
28	Thursday	○ FULL MOON
29	Friday	
30	Saturday	
31	Sunday	

2021

February
2021

JANUARY
S M T W T F S
1 2
3 4 5 6 7 8 9
10 11 12 13 14 15 16
17 18 19 20 21 22 23
24 25 26 27 28 29 30
31

MARCH
S M T W T F S
1 2 3 4 5 6
7 8 9 10 11 12 13
14 15 16 17 18 19 20
21 22 23 24 25 26 27
28 29 30 31

Sunday	Monday	Tuesday	Wednesday	Thursday	Friday	Saturday
31	1	2	3	4	5	6
		Groundhog Day				Waitangi Day (New Zealand)
7	8	9	10	11	12	13
	Waitangi Day (observed) (New Zealand)			● NEW MOON	Lincoln's Birthday / Chinese New Year	
14	15	16	17	18	19	20
Valentine's Day	Presidents' Day		Ash Wednesday			
21	22	23	24	25	26	27
	Washington's Birthday					○ FULL MOON
28	1	2	3	4	5	6

NOTES

Friendship takes the cake.

February

1	Monday	
2	Tuesday	Groundhog Day
3	Wednesday	
4	Thursday	
5	Friday	
6	Saturday	Waitangi Day (New Zealand)
7	Sunday	

2021

If you want to be the boss,
then start acting like the boss.

February

| 8 | Monday | Waitangi Day (observed) (New Zealand) |

| 9 | Tuesday | |

| 10 | Wednesday | |

| 11 | Thursday | ● NEW MOON |

| 12 | Friday | Lincoln's Birthday / Chinese New Year |

| 13 | Saturday | |

| 14 | Sunday | Valentine's Day |

2021

There's nothing you can't lick.

February

15	Monday	Presidents' Day
16	Tuesday	
17	Wednesday	Ash Wednesday
18	Thursday	
19	Friday	
20	Saturday	
21	Sunday	

2021

Life is a treasure best shared with friends.

_____
_____
_____
_____
_____
_____
_____
_____
_____
_____

February

| 22 | Monday | Washington's Birthday |

| 23 | Tuesday | |

| 24 | Wednesday | |

| 25 | Thursday | |

| 26 | Friday | |

| 27 | Saturday | ○ FULL MOON |

| 28 | Sunday | |

2021

March
2021

FEBRUARY
S M T W T F S
1 2 3 4 5 6
7 8 9 10 11 12 13
14 15 16 17 18 19 20
21 22 23 24 25 26 27
28

APRIL
S M T W T F S
1 2 3
4 5 6 7 8 9 10
11 12 13 14 15 16 17
18 19 20 21 22 23 24
25 26 27 28 29 30

Sunday	Monday	Tuesday	Wednesday	Thursday	Friday	Saturday
28	1 Labour Day (W. Australia)	2	3	4	5	6
7	8 International Women's Day Commonwealth Day (CAN, UK, AUS) Canberra Day (ACT) Labour Day (Victoria)	9	10	11	12	13 ● NEW MOON
14 Daylight Saving begins Mother's Day (UK)	15	16	17 St. Patrick's Day	18	19	20 Vernal Equinox
21	22	23	24	25	26	27 Passover begins at sundown
28 Palm Sunday ○ FULL MOON	29	30	31	1	2	3

NOTES

Nothing is as easy as it looks.

_____

_____

_____

_____

_____

_____

_____

_____

_____

_____

March

1	Monday	Labour Day (W. Australia)
2	Tuesday	
3	Wednesday	
4	Thursday	
5	Friday	
6	Saturday	
7	Sunday	

2021

Keep your eye on the prize.

_____
_____
_____
_____
_____
_____
_____
_____
_____
_____

March

8	Monday	International Women's Day
		Commonwealth Day (CAN, UK, Australia)
		Canberra Day (ACT)
		Labour Day (Victoria)

9	Tuesday	

10	Wednesday	

11	Thursday	

12	Friday	

13	Saturday	● NEW MOON

14	Sunday	Daylight Saving begins
		Mother's Day (UK)

2021

When life gets sour, a good friend
can make it sweeter.

March

15	Monday	

16	Tuesday	

17	Wednesday	St. Patrick's Day

18	Thursday	

19	Friday	

20	Saturday	Vernal Equinox

21	Sunday	

2021

Don't be greedy. Half of something is better than all of nothing.

March

22	Monday	
23	Tuesday	
24	Wednesday	
25	Thursday	
26	Friday	
27	Saturday	Passover begins at sundown
28	Sunday	Palm Sunday ○ FULL MOON

2021

April
2021

MARCH						
S	M	T	W	T	F	S
	1	2	3	4	5	6
7	8	9	10	11	12	13
14	15	16	17	18	19	20
21	22	23	24	25	26	27
28	29	30	31			

MAY						
S	M	T	W	T	F	S
						1
2	3	4	5	6	7	8
9	10	11	12	13	14	15
16	17	18	19	20	21	22
23	24	25	26	27	28	29
30	31					

Sunday	Monday	Tuesday	Wednesday	Thursday	Friday	Saturday
28	29	30	31	1	2 Good Friday	3
4 Easter Sunday	5 Easter Monday (CAN, UK, AUS, NZ)	6	7 Holocaust Remembrance Day begins at sundown	8	9	10
11 ● NEW MOON	12	13	14	15	16	17
18	19	20	21	22 Earth Day	23	24
25 ANZAC Day (Australia, NZ)	26 ANZAC Day (observed) (W. Australia, ACT) ○ FULL MOON	27	28	29	30 Arbor Day	1

If you've got a song to sing — sing it!

29	Monday	

30	Tuesday	

31	Wednesday	

1	Thursday	

2	Friday	Good Friday

3	Saturday	

4	Sunday	Easter Sunday

Superheroes come in
all shapes and sizes.

5 | Monday   Easter Monday
                                                  (CAN, UK, AUS, NZ)

6 | Tuesday

7 | Wednesday   Holocaust Remembrance Day
                                                  begins at sundown

8 | Thursday

9 | Friday

10 | Saturday

11 | Sunday   ● NEW MOON

Be ready to catch whatever
life throws your way.

April

12	Monday
13	Tuesday
14	Wednesday
15	Thursday
16	Friday
17	Saturday
18	Sunday

2021

We all need a little down time.

_____

_____

_____

_____

_____

_____

_____

_____

_____

April

19	Monday	
20	Tuesday	
21	Wednesday	
22	Thursday	Earth Day
23	Friday	
24	Saturday	
25	Sunday	ANZAC Day (Australia, NZ)

2021

May
2021

APRIL
S M T W T F S
1 2 3
4 5 6 7 8 9 10
11 12 13 14 15 16 17
18 19 20 21 22 23 24
25 26 27 28 29 30

JUNE
S M T W T F S
1 2 3 4 5
6 7 8 9 10 11 12
13 14 15 16 17 18 19
20 21 22 23 24 25 26
27 28 29 30

Sunday	Monday	Tuesday	Wednesday	Thursday	Friday	Saturday
25	26	27	28	29	30	1 May Day
2	3 Bank Holiday (UK) Labour Day (Queensland)	4	5	6	7	8
9 Mother's Day (US, CAN, AUS, NZ)	10	11 ● NEW MOON	12	13	14	15 Armed Forces Day
16	17	18	19	20	21	22
23/30	24/31 Victoria Day (24th) (Canada) Memorial Day (31st) Bank Holiday (31st) (UK)	25	26 ○ FULL MOON	27	28	29

NOTES

*Don't be afraid to be the light
of the party.*

26	Monday	ANZAC Day (observed) (W. Australia, ACT) ○ FULL MOON

27	Tuesday	

28	Wednesday	

29	Thursday	

30	Friday	Arbor Day

1	Saturday	May Day

2	Sunday	

2021

*Sometimes simply being there
is enough.*

_____

_____

_____

_____

_____

_____

_____

_____

_____

_____

May

3	Monday	<div align="right">Bank Holiday (UK) Labour Day (Queensland)</div>
4	Tuesday	
5	Wednesday	
6	Thursday	
7	Friday	
8	Saturday	
9	Sunday	<div align="right">Mother's Day (US, CAN, AUS, NZ)</div>

2021

*Picture yourself living the life
you've dreamt of.*

May

10	Monday	
11	Tuesday	● NEW MOON
12	Wednesday	
13	Thursday	
14	Friday	
15	Saturday	Armed Forces Day
16	Sunday	

2021

Sometimes you just gotta suck it up.

May

17	Monday
18	Tuesday
19	Wednesday
20	Thursday
21	Friday
22	Saturday
23	Sunday

2021

Happiness comes in waves —
take time to enjoy the ride!

May

24	Monday	Victoria Day (Canada)

25	Tuesday	

26	Wednesday	○ FULL MOON

27	Thursday	

28	Friday	

29	Saturday	

30	Sunday	

2021

June
2021

MAY
S M T W T F S
                1
2 3 4 5 6 7 8
9 10 11 12 13 14 15
16 17 18 19 20 21 22
23 24 25 26 27 28 29
30 31

JULY
S M T W T F S
          1 2 3
4 5 6 7 8 9 10
11 12 13 14 15 16 17
18 19 20 21 22 23 24
25 26 27 28 29 30 31

Sunday	Monday	Tuesday	Wednesday	Thursday	Friday	Saturday
30	31	1	2	3	4	5
6	7 Queen's Birthday (New Zealand)	8	9	10 ● NEW MOON	11	12
13	14 Flag Day Queen's Birthday (Australia)	15	16	17	18	19
20 Summer Solstice Father's Day (US, Canada, UK)	21	22	23	24 ○ FULL MOON	25	26
27	28	29	30	1	2	3

NOTES

Life is short. Make a big splash!

_____
_____
_____
_____
_____
_____
_____
_____
_____
_____
_____

| 31 | Monday | Memorial Day
Bank Holiday
(UK) |

| 1 | Tuesday | |

| 2 | Wednesday | |

| 3 | Thursday | |

| 4 | Friday | |

| 5 | Saturday | |

| 6 | Sunday | |

2021

When you are in deep, don't flip out.

June

7	Monday	Queen's Birthday (New Zealand)
8	Tuesday	
9	Wednesday	
10	Thursday	● NEW MOON
11	Friday	
12	Saturday	
13	Sunday	

2021

Shake things up every once in a while.

June

| 14 | Monday | Flag Day
Queen's Birthday
(Australia) |

| 15 | Tuesday | |

| 16 | Wednesday | |

| 17 | Thursday | |

| 18 | Friday | |

| 19 | Saturday | |

| 20 | Sunday | Summer Solstice
Father's Day
(US, Canada, UK) |

2021

Know when to go with the flow.

June

21 | Monday

22 | Tuesday

23 | Wednesday

24 | Thursday   ○ FULL MOON

25 | Friday

26 | Saturday

27 | Sunday

2021

July
2021

JUNE
S M T W T F S
1 2 3 4 5
6 7 8 9 10 11 12
13 14 15 16 17 18 19
20 21 22 23 24 25 26
27 28 29 30

AUGUST
S M T W T F S
1 2 3 4 5 6 7
8 9 10 11 12 13 14
15 16 17 18 19 20 21
22 23 24 25 26 27 28
29 30 31

Sunday	Monday	Tuesday	Wednesday	Thursday	Friday	Saturday
27	28	29	30	1 Canada Day	2	3
4 Independence Day	5	6	7	8	9 ● NEW MOON	10
11	12	13	14	15	16	17
18	19	20	21	22	23 ○ FULL MOON	24
25	26	27	28	29	30	31

NOTES

Sometimes you just have to take the plunge and hope for the best.

28	Monday	
29	Tuesday	
30	Wednesday	
1	Thursday	Canada Day
2	Friday	
3	Saturday	
4	Sunday	Independence Day

2021

Keep cool and carry on.

July

5	Monday

6	Tuesday

7	Wednesday

8	Thursday

9	Friday	● NEW MOON

10	Saturday

11	Sunday

2021

Photographs © 2020 Ron Schmidt

A well-rounded life is all about balance.

July

12 | Monday

13 | Tuesday

14 | Wednesday

15 | Thursday

16 | Friday

17 | Saturday

18 | Sunday

2021

Everyone has their own song to sing.

July

19	Monday
20	Tuesday
21	Wednesday
22	Thursday
23	Friday ○ FULL MOON
24	Saturday
25	Sunday

2021

August
2021

JULY
S M T W T F S
1 2 3
4 5 6 7 8 9 10
11 12 13 14 15 16 17
18 19 20 21 22 23 24
25 26 27 28 29 30 31

SEPTEMBER
S M T W T F S
1 2 3 4
5 6 7 8 9 10 11
12 13 14 15 16 17 18
19 20 21 22 23 24 25
26 27 28 29 30

Sunday	Monday	Tuesday	Wednesday	Thursday	Friday	Saturday
1	2 Civic Holiday (Canada) Bank Holiday (NSW)	3	4	5	6	7
8 ● NEW MOON	9	10	11	12	13	14
15	16	17	18	19	20	21
22 ○ FULL MOON	23	24	25	26	27	28
29	30 Bank Holiday (UK)	31	1	2	3	4

We can't control the wind,
but we can adjust the sails.

26	Monday

27	Tuesday

28	Wednesday

29	Thursday

30	Friday

31	Saturday

1	Sunday

*Never be afraid to bite off
more than you can chew.*

August

2	Monday

Civic Holiday
(Canada)
Bank Holiday
(NSW)

3 | Tuesday

4 | Wednesday

5 | Thursday

6 | Friday

7 | Saturday

8 | Sunday

● NEW MOON

2021

Keep an eye on the fruits of your labor.

August

9	Monday
10	Tuesday
11	Wednesday
12	Thursday
13	Friday
14	Saturday
15	Sunday

2021

Whether you think you can, or you think you can't, you're right.

August

16	Monday

17	Tuesday

18	Wednesday

19	Thursday

20	Friday

21	Saturday

22	Sunday	○ FULL MOON

2021

Temptation is everywhere.
Weigh your options.

August

23	Monday
24	Tuesday
25	Wednesday
26	Thursday
27	Friday
28	Saturday
29	Sunday

2021

September
2021

AUGUST
S M T W T F S
1 2 3 4 5 6 7
8 9 10 11 12 13 14
15 16 17 18 19 20 21
22 23 24 25 26 27 28
29 30 31

OCTOBER
S M T W T F S
1 2
3 4 5 6 7 8 9
10 11 12 13 14 15 16
17 18 19 20 21 22 23
24 25 26 27 28 29 30
31

Sunday	Monday	Tuesday	Wednesday	Thursday	Friday	Saturday
29	30	31	1	2	3	4
5 Father's Day (Australia, NZ)	6 Rosh Hashanah begins at sundown Labor Day (US, Canada) ● NEW MOON	7	8	9	10	11
12	13	14	15 Yom Kippur begins at sundown	16	17	18
19	20 ○ FULL MOON	21 UN International Day of Peace	22 Autumnal Equinox	23	24	25
26	27 Queen's Birthday (W. Australia)	28	29	30	1	2

NOTES

Hang tight and good things
will come to you.

30	Monday	Bank Holiday (UK)
31	Tuesday	
1	Wednesday	
2	Thursday	
3	Friday	
4	Saturday	
5	Sunday	Father's Day (Australia, NZ)

2021

Never underestimate the power
of a smart hat.

September

6	Monday	Rosh Hashanah begins at sundown Labor Day (US, Canada) ● NEW MOON
7	Tuesday	
8	Wednesday	
9	Thursday	
10	Friday	
11	Saturday	
12	Sunday	

2021

Live the life you've imagined!

September

13	Monday
14	Tuesday
15	Wednesday — Yom Kippur begins at sundown
16	Thursday
17	Friday
18	Saturday
19	Sunday

2021

Each of us has our own journey.

_____

_____

_____

_____

_____

_____

_____

_____

_____

_____

_____

September

20	Monday	○ FULL MOON

21	Tuesday	UN International Day of Peace

22	Wednesday	Autumnal Equinox

23	Thursday	

24	Friday	

25	Saturday	

26	Sunday	

2021

October
2021

SEPTEMBER
S M T W T F S
            1 2 3 4
5 6 7 8 9 10 11
12 13 14 15 16 17 18
19 20 21 22 23 24 25
26 27 28 29 30

NOVEMBER
S M T W T F S
   1 2 3 4 5 6
7 8 9 10 11 12 13
14 15 16 17 18 19 20
21 22 23 24 25 26 27
28 29 30

Sunday	Monday	Tuesday	Wednesday	Thursday	Friday	Saturday
26	27	28	29	30	1	2
3	4 Labour Day (ACT, NSW, SA) Queen's Birthday (Queensland)	5	6 ● NEW MOON	7	8	9
10	11 Columbus Day (observed) Thanksgiving (Canada) Indigenous Peoples' Day (observed)	12	13	14	15	16
17	18	19	20 ○ FULL MOON	21	22	23
24/31 Halloween (31st)	25 Labour Day (New Zealand)	26	27	28	29	30

Cleanliness is next to dog-li-ness.

_____

_____

_____

_____

_____

_____

_____

_____

_____

_____

| 27 | Monday | Queen's Birthday
(W. Australia) |

| 28 | Tuesday | |

| 29 | Wednesday | |

| 30 | Thursday | |

| 1 | Friday | |

| 2 | Saturday | |

| 3 | Sunday | |

2021

When life hands you sour grapes,
just roll with it.

_____

_____

_____

_____

_____

_____

_____

_____

_____

October

4	Monday	Labour Day (ACT, NSW, SA)
		Queen's Birthday (Queensland)

5	Tuesday

6	Wednesday	● NEW MOON

7	Thursday

8	Friday

9	Saturday

10	Sunday

2021

Heads or tails —
life is what you make it.

_____

_____

_____

_____

_____

_____

_____

_____

_____

October

11	Monday	Columbus Day (observed) Thanksgiving (Canada) Indigenous Peoples' Day (observed)
12	Tuesday	
13	Wednesday	
14	Thursday	
15	Friday	
16	Saturday	
17	Sunday	

2021

Determination brings great rewards.

October

18	Monday

19	Tuesday

20	Wednesday	○ FULL MOON

21	Thursday

22	Friday

23	Saturday

24	Sunday

2021

Try seeing things from someone else's point of view every now and again.

October

25	Monday	Labour Day (New Zealand)
26	Tuesday	
27	Wednesday	
28	Thursday	
29	Friday	
30	Saturday	
31	Sunday	Halloween

2021

November
2021

OCTOBER
S M T W T F S
1 2
3 4 5 6 7 8 9
10 11 12 13 14 15 16
17 18 19 20 21 22 23
24 25 26 27 28 29 30
31

DECEMBER
S M T W T F S
1 2 3 4
5 6 7 8 9 10 11
12 13 14 15 16 17 18
19 20 21 22 23 24 25
26 27 28 29 30 31

Sunday	Monday	Tuesday	Wednesday	Thursday	Friday	Saturday
31	1 All Saints' Day	2 Election Day	3	4 ● NEW MOON	5	6
7 Daylight Saving ends	8	9	10	11 Veterans Day Remembrance Day (CAN, AUS, NZ)	12	13
14 Remembrance Sunday (UK)	15	16	17	18	19 ○ FULL MOON	20
21	22	23	24	25 Thanksgiving	26	27
28 Hanukkah begins at sundown	29	30	1	2	3	4

NOTES

Better to have one of something
than all of nothing.

November

1	Monday	All Saints' Day
2	Tuesday	Election Day
3	Wednesday	
4	Thursday	● NEW MOON
5	Friday	
6	Saturday	
7	Sunday	Daylight Saving ends

2021

Go someplace you've never been before.

November

8	Monday

9	Tuesday

10	Wednesday

11	Thursday	Veterans Day
		Remembrance Day (CAN, AUS, NZ)

12	Friday

13	Saturday

14	Sunday	Remembrance Sunday (UK)

2021

Take pride in where you come from.

_____

_____

_____

_____

_____

_____

_____

_____

_____

November

15	Monday

16	Tuesday

17	Wednesday

18	Thursday

19	Friday	○ FULL MOON

20	Saturday

21	Sunday

2021

Nothing is really out of reach.

November

22	Monday	
23	Tuesday	
24	Wednesday	
25	Thursday	Thanksgiving
26	Friday	
27	Saturday	
28	Sunday	Hanukkah begins at sundown

2021

December
2021

NOVEMBER						
S	M	T	W	T	F	S
	1	2	3	4	5	6
7	8	9	10	11	12	13
14	15	16	17	18	19	20
21	22	23	24	25	26	27
28	29	30				

JANUARY 2022						
S	M	T	W	T	F	S
						1
2	3	4	5	6	7	8
9	10	11	12	13	14	15
16	17	18	19	20	21	22
23	24	25	26	27	28	29
30	31					

Sunday	Monday	Tuesday	Wednesday	Thursday	Friday	Saturday
28	29	30	1	2	3	4 ● NEW MOON
5	6	7 Pearl Harbor Remembrance Day	8	9	10	11
12	13	14	15	16	17	18 ○ FULL MOON
19	20	21 Winter Solstice	22	23	24	25 Christmas
26 Boxing Day (CAN, UK, AUS, NZ) Kwanzaa begins	27 Boxing Day (observed) (CAN, UK, AUS, NZ)	28	29	30	31	1

NOTES

Good things come to those who wait.

29	Monday

30	Tuesday

1	Wednesday

2	Thursday

3	Friday

4	Saturday	● NEW MOON

5	Sunday

Know the difference between being in deep and being in over your head.

December

6	Monday

7	Tuesday	Pearl Harbor Remembrance Day

8	Wednesday

9	Thursday

10	Friday

11	Saturday

12	Sunday

2021

Imagination is the key ingredient
to a happy life.

December

13	Monday
14	Tuesday
15	Wednesday
16	Thursday
17	Friday
18	Saturday ○ FULL MOON
19	Sunday

2021

Life is short. Enjoy the ride.

December

20	Monday	

21	Tuesday	Winter Solstice

22	Wednesday	

23	Thursday	

24	Friday	

25	Saturday	Christmas

26	Sunday	Boxing Day (CAN, UK, AUS, NZ) Kwanzaa begins

2021

True peace is found in a balanced life.

December/
January 2022

27	Monday	<div align="right">Boxing Day (observed) (CAN, UK, AUS, NZ)</div>

28	Tuesday	

29	Wednesday	

30	Thursday	

31	Friday	

1	Saturday	New Year's Day

2	Sunday	● NEW MOON

2021

January
2022

DECEMBER
S M T W T F S
1 2 3 4
5 6 7 8 9 10 11
12 13 14 15 16 17 18
19 20 21 22 23 24 25
26 27 28 29 30 31

FEBRUARY
S M T W T F S
1 2 3 4 5
6 7 8 9 10 11 12
13 14 15 16 17 18 19
20 21 22 23 24 25 26
27 28

Sunday	Monday	Tuesday	Wednesday	Thursday	Friday	Saturday
26	27	28	29	30	31	1 New Year's Day
2 ● NEW MOON	3	4	5	6	7	8
9	10	11	12	13	14	15 Martin Luther King Jr.'s Birthday
16	17 Martin Luther King Jr.'s Birthday (observed) ○ FULL MOON	18	19	20	21	22
23/30	24/31	25	26 Australia Day	27	28	29

NOTES

2022

JANUARY

S	M	T	W	T	F	S
						1
2	3	4	5	6	7	8
9	10	11	12	13	14	15
16	17	18	19	20	21	22
23	24	25	26	27	28	29
30	31					

FEBRUARY

S	M	T	W	T	F	S
		1	2	3	4	5
6	7	8	9	10	11	12
13	14	15	16	17	18	19
20	21	22	23	24	25	26
27	28					

MARCH

S	M	T	W	T	F	S
		1	2	3	4	5
6	7	8	9	10	11	12
13	14	15	16	17	18	19
20	21	22	23	24	25	26
27	28	29	30	31		

APRIL

S	M	T	W	T	F	S
					1	2
3	4	5	6	7	8	9
10	11	12	13	14	15	16
17	18	19	20	21	22	23
24	25	26	27	28	29	30

MAY

S	M	T	W	T	F	S
1	2	3	4	5	6	7
8	9	10	11	12	13	14
15	16	17	18	19	20	21
22	23	24	25	26	27	28
29	30	31				

JUNE

S	M	T	W	T	F	S
			1	2	3	4
5	6	7	8	9	10	11
12	13	14	15	16	17	18
19	20	21	22	23	24	25
26	27	28	29	30		

JULY

S	M	T	W	T	F	S
					1	2
3	4	5	6	7	8	9
10	11	12	13	14	15	16
17	18	19	20	21	22	23
24	25	26	27	28	29	30
31						

AUGUST

S	M	T	W	T	F	S
	1	2	3	4	5	6
7	8	9	10	11	12	13
14	15	16	17	18	19	20
21	22	23	24	25	26	27
28	29	30	31			

SEPTEMBER

S	M	T	W	T	F	S
				1	2	3
4	5	6	7	8	9	10
11	12	13	14	15	16	17
18	19	20	21	22	23	24
25	26	27	28	29	30	

OCTOBER

S	M	T	W	T	F	S
						1
2	3	4	5	6	7	8
9	10	11	12	13	14	15
16	17	18	19	20	21	22
23	24	25	26	27	28	29
30	31					

NOVEMBER

S	M	T	W	T	F	S
		1	2	3	4	5
6	7	8	9	10	11	12
13	14	15	16	17	18	19
20	21	22	23	24	25	26
27	28	29	30			

DECEMBER

S	M	T	W	T	F	S
				1	2	3
4	5	6	7	8	9	10
11	12	13	14	15	16	17
18	19	20	21	22	23	24
25	26	27	28	29	30	31

JANUARY

- _____
- _____
- _____
- _____
- _____
- _____

FEBRUARY

- _____
- _____
- _____
- _____
- _____
- _____

MARCH

- _____
- _____
- _____
- _____
- _____
- _____

APRIL

- _____
- _____
- _____
- _____
- _____
- _____

MAY

- _____
- _____
- _____
- _____
- _____
- _____

JUNE

- _____
- _____
- _____
- _____
- _____
- _____

JULY

- _____
- _____
- _____
- _____
- _____
- _____

AUGUST

- _____
- _____
- _____
- _____
- _____
- _____

SEPTEMBER

- _____
- _____
- _____
- _____
- _____
- _____

OCTOBER

- _____
- _____
- _____
- _____
- _____
- _____

NOVEMBER

- _____
- _____
- _____
- _____
- _____
- _____

DECEMBER

- _____
- _____
- _____
- _____
- _____
- _____

NOTES

NOTES

NOTES

NOTES

NOTES

RON
SCHMIDT
WWW.LOOSELEASHES.COM

SELLERS
PUBLISHING

For more information
regarding this and other products:
WWW.MAKEFUN.COM I RSP@RSVP.COM

Canadian Stores Contact: Andrew Shapiro
(800) 625-3386 I ASHAPIRO@RSVP.COM

ISBN 13: 978-1-5319-1162-1
Printed in China with soy-based inks.

Astronomical information is in Eastern Time and Daylight Saving Time.
Key to abbreviations: United States (US), Canada (CAN), United Kingdom (UK), Australia (AUS), South Australia (SA),
Western Australia (W. Australia), New South Wales (NSW), Australian Capital Territory (ACT), New Zealand (NZ).